HOW'S YOUR HEALTH?

Head Lice

Angela Royston

Smart Apple Media

Smart Apple Media is published by Black Rabbit Books
P.O. Box 3263, Mankato, Minnesota 56002

Printed in the United States

Published by arrangement with the Watts Publishing Group Ltd, London.

Editor: Sarah Eason
Design: Paul Myerscough
Illustration: Annie Boberg and Geoff Ward
Photo research: Sarah Jameson
Consultant: Dr. Stephen Earwicker

Acknowledgements:
The publisher would like to thank the following for permission to reproduce photographs: Alamy p.6, p.8, p.11, p.16; Corbis p.22; Inmagine p.7, p.17, p.27; Tudor Photography p.7, p.12, p.14, p.18, p.24, p.26; Chris Fairclough Photography p.13, p.15, p.19, p.20, p.21, p.23, p.25.

Library of Congress Cataloging-in-Publication Data

Royston, Angela.
    Head lice / Angela Royston.
    p. cm.—(Smart Apple Media. How's your health?)
    Summary: "Describes the causes, symptoms, and treatment of head lice and how to prevent yourself from getting them"—Provided by publisher.
    Includes index.
    ISBN-13: 978-1-59920-218-1
    1. Pediculosis—Juvenile literature. I. Title.
RL764.P4R692 2009
616.5'72—dc22   2007035703

9 8 7 6 5 4 3 2 1

Contents

What Are Head Lice?

Head lice are tiny insects that live in your hair. They also lay eggs in your hair.

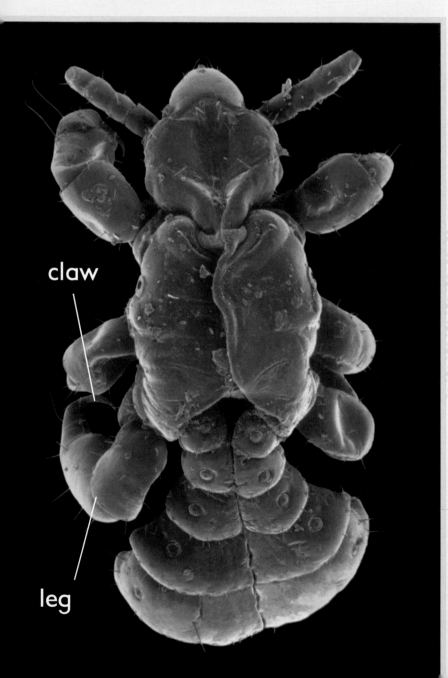

claw

leg

A head **louse** is only about ¹/₁₀ of an inch (3 mm) long. This head louse has been **magnified** so that it looks much bigger. It has six legs with a claw at the end of each leg.

Head lice live in both clean and dirty hair. It is difficult to see them because they are so small and move so quickly through hair. Head lice are annoying because they make your **scalp** itch.

Tiny Pests

A head louse is only the same size as this dot! •

Why Do Head Lice Like Hair?

Head lice bite the skin on your head to feed on your blood. They can also lay their eggs in your hair.

A head louse cannot jump or fly. Instead, it uses its claws to cling to hair. It clings so tightly that it cannot be shaken off.

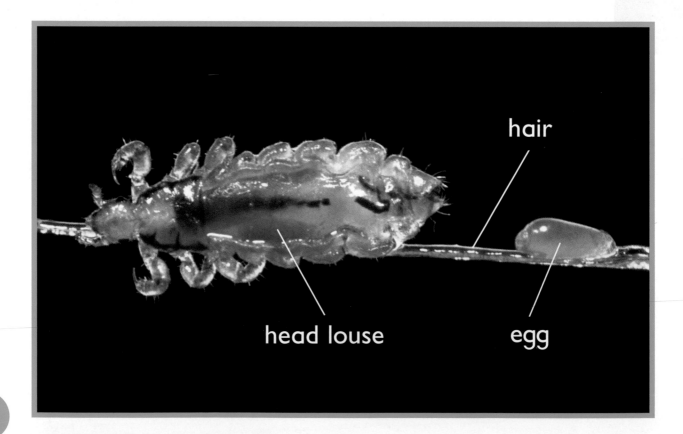

hair

head louse

egg

Head lice lay most of their eggs in the hair behind your ears and at your neck. They glue each egg to a hair about $\frac{1}{3}$ of an inch (1 cm) from your scalp.

hair

egg

Hundreds of Eggs

A female head louse can live up to 40 days. She lays about six eggs a day and as many as 240 eggs before she dies!

What Are Nits?

Baby head lice grow inside eggs laid by female adult lice. The baby lice and their eggs are called **nits**.

head louse

Once a young head louse has **hatched** from its egg, it crawls to the scalp. There it feeds and grows until it becomes an adult. If it is female, then it is ready to make its own eggs.

egg

10

Super Babies

A young louse hatches about eight days after its egg was laid. It feeds on blood and grows for just 9 to 12 days. Female lice then begin to lay eggs.

After a louse has hatched from its egg, the empty eggshell remains glued to the hair. It is a pearly white color.

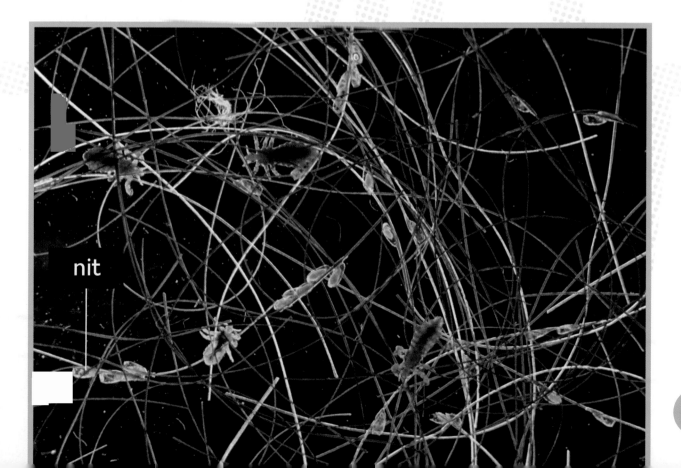

nit

How Do You Know if You Have Head Lice?

Most people with head lice have an itchy head. If your head is itchy, ask an adult to look for nits in your hair.

When a head louse bites your scalp, the bite can make your scalp itch. However, some people do not get an itchy scalp right away. Others never get an itchy scalp.

The best way to find out if someone has head lice is to look for nits. Hair should be checked while it is combed with a fine-toothed comb.

Other Things That Can Make Your Head Itch

+ Dirty hair
+ Using a shampoo that isn't best for your hair type
+ **Dandruff**
+ **Mites** or insects that have landed in your hair

How Do People Get Head Lice?

People catch head lice from other people who have them.

If someone's hair brushes against another person's hair, head lice can quickly move from one head to the other.

Head lice can move from hair onto other things, such as hats. They can live there for a few hours before crawling onto someone else's scalp.

Other Ways Head Lice Can Be Caught

+ Wearing someone else's hat
+ Cuddling a furry toy
+ Using someone else's hairbrush or comb
+ Lying on someone else's pillow

If one person in a family has head lice, the lice could soon spread to everyone else in the family.

Who Gets Head Lice?

Anyone with hair can catch head lice. Only people with no hair at all cannot catch head lice.

Children ages 5 and 6 are most likely to catch head lice. Young children are more likely to touch heads with someone else than adults or older children.

African Americans with very curly hair are less likely to catch head lice. The lice cannot move through their hair as easily as they can through straighter hair.

How Can You Get Rid of Head Lice?

Special shampoos or **olive oil** kill head lice. Olive oil is gentler to your skin than special shampoos.

Normal shampoo does not kill head lice. Only special shampoo for head lice will kill them. Some special shampoos use **herbs** to get rid of the lice. Others use strong **chemicals**.

You can also kill head lice by combing olive oil through your hair. The oil stops the lice from breathing. Leave the oil in your hair overnight and wash it out with normal shampoo the next morning.

Take Care!

The chemicals in special shampoos are very strong. Make sure you do not get them in your eyes or mouth. Only use the shampoo if you are sure you have head lice.

What Is a Nit Comb?

A **nit comb** is a comb that has teeth so close together that they trap lice between them.

Once head lice have been killed with shampoo or olive oil, they can be combed out of the hair with a nit comb. The hair must be treated again with shampoo or olive oil two weeks later to kill any newly hatched lice.

Getting Rid of Eggs

Treating hair with shampoo or olive oil will not kill eggs that have already been laid. The hair must be treated again two weeks later. By this time the eggs will have hatched, but the lice inside will not have laid their own eggs.

This nit comb kills lice with an **electric shock**. If you use an electric nit comb there is no need to use a special shampoo or olive oil. However, the electric nit comb must be used often to kill all the lice.

How Can You Stop Head Lice from Spreading?

If you have head lice, then your friends and family should also treat their hair for lice.

The only way to stop lice from spreading through a family is for all family members to treat their hair for lice. They must all use a special shampoo or olive oil at the same time.

The only way to stop lice from spreading through a class or school is for everyone to treat their hair for lice on the same evening. The school will tell children which night they should treat their hair.

Louse Busting!

After washing your hair, have a parent comb the wet hair with a fine nit comb for about half an hour. Repeat this every three to four days. Continue for two weeks until you have combed out the last louse.

Can You Prevent Head Lice?

No one can stop head lice from moving into their hair. This is why you should keep checking for nits and lice.

It is difficult to see head lice in someone's hair. It is much easier to see nits. Parents and caregivers should check their children's hair regularly.

How Can You Tell Nits from Dandruff?

Many people have little white specks in their hair. This is usually a sign of dandruff. The white specks are flakes of skin. Unlike nits, it is easy to brush or shake dandruff from your hair.

After you wash your hair, comb it with a nit comb while your hair is still wet. After each stroke, look to see if you have caught a louse. If you do find one, tell your teacher or your mom or dad.

Can Tidy Hair Stop You from Catching Head Lice?

Your hair is less likely to touch someone else's hair if it is tidy.

Braiding hair is a good way to keep it tidy. Long hair can also be tied back into a ponytail.

People with short hair catch head lice just as easily as people with long hair. However, it is easier to check short hair for nits.

How You Can Help

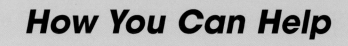

+ Tie back long hair with clips or a hair band.
+ Avoid touching heads with other people.
+ Avoid using other people's hats, hairbrushes, and pillows.

Glossary

chemical powerful substance found in many man-made things, including cleaning supplies and beauty products.

dandruff flakes of dry skin that have fallen from the scalp.

electric shock shock caused by electricity.

hatch when a baby animal or insect breaks out of its egg.

herb plant that is used in cooking or medicines.

louse insect that lives in hair. More than one are called lice.

magnified made to look much bigger.

mite very small spider-like animal.

nit louse egg and the baby louse that hatches from it.

nit comb comb with teeth set very close together. Nits and lice are caught between the teeth.

olive oil liquid made from crushed olives and usually used for cooking.

scalp skin that covers your head and from which your hair grows.

Find Out More

For Kids: Lice Aren't So Nice
www.kidshealth.org/kid/ill_injure/sick/lice.html

Headlice.org for Kids: Games, Frequently Asked Questions, and More
www.headlice.org/kids/

Head Lice Treatments for Children
www.keepkidshealthy.com/welcome/treatmentguides/lice.html

Every effort has been made by the publisher to ensure that these Web sites contain no inappropriate or offensive material. However, because of the nature of the Internet, it is impossible to guarantee that the contents of these sites will not be altered. We strongly advise that Internet access is supervised by a responsible adult.

Index

ML

10/08